Fact Finders®

Explore the Biomes

EXPLORE THE

Tundra

by Linda Tagliaferro

Consultant:
Dr. Sandra Mather
Professor Emerita of Geology and Astronomy
West Chester University
West Chester, Pennsylvania

Capstone
press®

Mankato, Minnesota

F...
151 Good Co...   56002.

Library of Congress Cataloging-in-Publication Data
Tagliaferro, Linda.
    Explore the tundra / by Linda Tagliaferro.
    p. cm. —(Fact finders. Explore the biomes)
    Includes bibliographical references and index.
    ISBN-13: 978-0-7368-6408-4 (hardcover)
    ISBN-10: 0-7368-6408-3 (hardcover)
    ISBN-13: 978-0-7368-9631-3 (softcover pbk.)
    ISBN-10: 0-7368-9631-7 (softcover pbk.)
    1. Tundra ecology—Juvenile literature. I. Title. II. Series.
QH541.5.T8T34 2007
577.5′86—dc22   2006004108

Summary: Discusses the plants, animals, and characteristics of the tundra biome.

Editorial Credits
Erika L. Shores, editor; Juliette Peters, designer; Tami Collins, illustrator; Wanda Winch, photo researcher

Photo Credits
Accent Alaska/Barbara Brundege, 12; Hugh Rose, 22–23
Ardea/Andrey Zvoznikoy, 11
Cheryl A. Ertelt, cover (background), 6 (top), 15, 16 (right)
Corbis/Richard Cummins, 25 (sign)
Courtesy of Linda Tagliaferro, 32
Creatas, 1 (mosquito)
Department of Geography, University of Cincinnati, 29 (both)
Getty Images Inc./The Image Bank/David W. Hamilton, cover (foreground)
The Image Works/Syracuse Newspapers, 25
Minden Pictures/Michio Hoshino, 4–5, 8–9, 13
Nature Picture Library/Brian Lightfoot, 10–11
Peter Arnold/Klein, 16 (top); Michael Sewell, 20–21; S. J. Krasemann, 17, 24
Photodisc/Siede Preis, 1 (rock), 3
Shutterstock, 23, 27; Halldor Eiriksson, 19; James R. Hearn, 14; Nathalie Speliers Ufermann, 12–13 (mosquitoes); Nelson Sirlin, 4; Romeo Koitmae, 6 (bottom right)
Tom & Pat Leeson, 18

1 2 3 4 5 6 11 10 09 08 07 06

Table of Contents

CHAPTER 1

A Frozen Land

The wind howls across a frozen land. Close to the ground, small plants with bright yellow and red flowers sway in the wind. A caribou munches on short grass.

Near the North Pole lies one of the coldest places on earth, called the tundra. Little snow or rain falls throughout the year. Few plants and animals can survive in the **harsh** conditions of this frozen desert.

Short plants and tough caribou manage to thrive on the windy, dry tundra.

The Tundra Biome

Together, plants and animals make up a community called a **biome**. Because of its unique **climate,** each biome has types of plants and animals that don't live anywhere else on earth. The plants and animals that live on the tundra are suited to its climate.

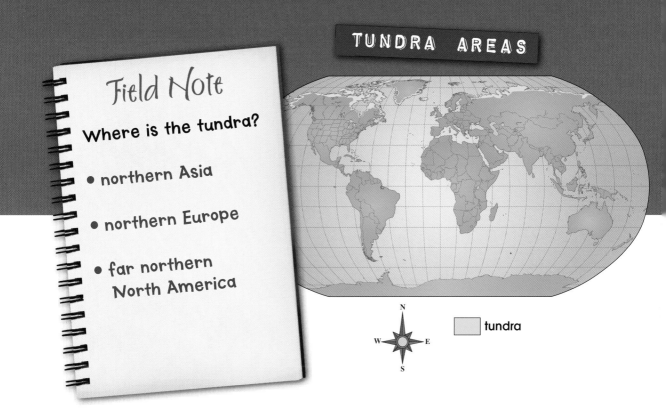

Field Note

Where is the tundra?

- northern Asia

- northern Europe

- far northern North America

TUNDRA AREAS

tundra

The tundra biome is made up of extremely cold, mostly flat land that lies along an imaginary line called the **Arctic Circle**. Tundra winters are long and harsh. Winds blow and snow covers the frozen ground. In winter, the tundra gets little sunlight and stays dark for weeks. During short tundra summers, the sun shines almost 24 hours each day.

CHAPTER 2

Tundra Plants and Animals in Summer

In the mild summer, tundra snow melts, but only the top layer of soil gets warm. Beneath the top layer, the ground stays frozen. Trees can't live where this **permafrost** exists because their long roots can't grow in the frozen soil. Many tundra plants have short roots so they can live in the shallow topsoil.

Moss and other small plants grow close to the ground in large groups. Plants on the edge of the group protect the middle plants from strong winds. Lichens are plants without roots. They live by attaching themselves to rocks.

Arctic poppies grow close to the ground. The flowers follow the sun as it crosses the sky.

FACT!

The growing season in the tundra lasts just 50 to 60 days.

Food on the Tundra

Food is scarce on the tundra, except in summer. Plants grow quickly because they receive 24 hours of sunlight. People can find blueberries and bilberries to eat. Orange berries called cloudberries grow only on the tundra.

When tundra birds eat berries, they swallow the tiny seeds. Then birds fly away. When they pass waste, the seeds spread to other places. Birds help new plants grow all over the tundra.

Cloudberries start out red and turn orange as they ripen.

Other animals find plenty of food to eat on the tundra in summer. Arctic hares nibble on mosses and lichens. Tiny lemmings use their claws to dig up plant roots.

Field Note

Lemmings:
- Size: size of a small mouse
- Color: brown, gray; some kinds are white in winter
- Habitat: burrows; builds winter nests of grasses on the ground
- Food: roots, grasses

Insects on the Tundra

In summer, melting snow on the tundra can't sink deep into the frozen permafrost. Water collects near the top of the soil and shallow lakes and ponds form. Shallow ponds are good places for mosquitoes to lay eggs. The buzzing of millions of mosquitoes fills the air in summer.

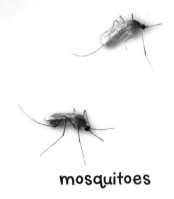

mosquitoes

Female mosquitoes lay eggs in ponds formed when tundra snow melts.

Hundreds of buzzing mosquitoes swarm around a moose.

Birds think of mosquitoes as tasty snacks. Mosquitoes think the same of tundra animals. Mosquitoes need blood from other animals in order to lay their eggs.

Other insects live on the tundra in summer. Black flies and deer flies are also food for tundra birds.

FACT!

Mosquitoes don't freeze in winter because the water in their bodies is replaced with a chemical called glycerol. Mosquitoes live under the snow until the weather turns warm in summer.

CHAPTER 3

Tundra Plants and Animals in Winter

In winter, the tundra sky darkens, and the temperature drops far below freezing. Tundra plants and animals have adapted to cope with frigid weather. Sap does not freeze in tundra plants in winter. If the sap froze, plant stems would burst. Some plants stay alive as seeds during winter. They sprout when the weather is warmer.

Animals have ways to keep warm in winter. Polar bears and wolves have thick fur. Musk oxen have a layer of woolly fur next to their bodies to keep heat in. They also have an outer layer of long fur that protects against wind and snow. Ptarmigans and other tundra birds have feathers that keep out water.

gray wolf

The ptarmigan even has feathers on its feet to keep it warm during winter.

An arctic fox does not stay brown all year. Its fur turns white in winter.

Tundra Animals Change Color

Weather on the tundra affects animals in other ways. **Ermines** and arctic foxes are white in winter. Their color blends in with the snow. That way they can sneak up on prey. In summer, when plants are plentiful, ermines and arctic foxes turn brown.

arctic fox in winter

16

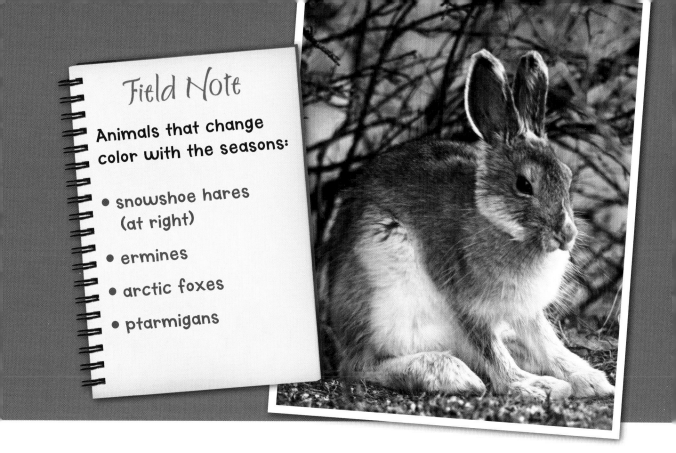

Field Note

Animals that change color with the seasons:

- snowshoe hares (at right)
- ermines
- arctic foxes
- ptarmigans

Changing fur color also keeps animals safe. Snowy owls hunt ermines. In winter, ermines are white, so it's hard for the owls to spot them in the snow. In summer, snowshoe hares and other white animals turn brown. It is harder for arctic wolves to see them among the tundra plants.

When the weather starts to turn colder, caribou head south to warmer areas.

Away for the Winter

Not all animals can survive on the tundra year-round. Some **migrate**, or travel, to warmer places to escape the frozen winter. In summer, they return to the tundra. Huge herds of caribou come to the tundra when it's warm. They raise their young there and leave again when the temperature falls and food is hard to find.

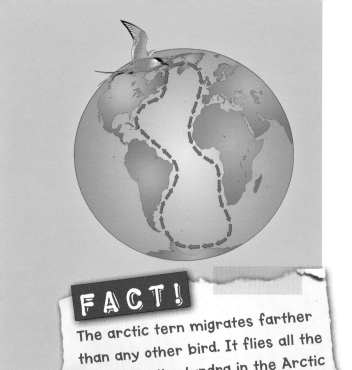

Many tundra birds fly south to find food in winter. Arctic terns leave the tundra for areas in the southern part of the world. The birds return to the tundra in spring to mate. They feed on insects and fish during summer.

CHAPTER 4

People and the Tundra

The sun shines on the shimmering blue water. A man with a fishing rod waits for a bite. The man is one of the Inuit people who live on the tundra. These native people catch trout, whitefish, and other fish in tundra lakes and streams. They also hunt caribou and whales.

The Inuit respect the land. They only hunt and fish for the food they need. But changes in the earth's climate have affected the Inuits' daily lives. Warmer temperatures cause tundra ice to melt. The melting ice makes it harder for the animals hunted by the Inuit to survive on the tundra.

Inuit people have followed their way of life on the tundra for thousands of years.

Harming the Tundra

Some people affect the tundra in negative ways. Factories, cars, and homes burn coal and oil that give off **pollution**. Winds push the polluting gases north to the tundra. The gases kill tundra plants and make it hard for animals to find food.

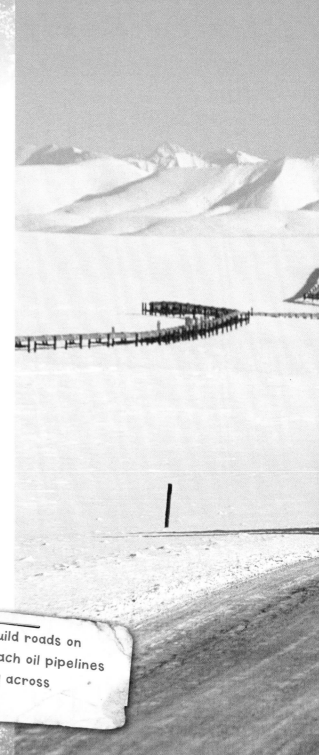

Oil companies build roads on the tundra to reach oil pipelines (far left) running across the land.

Oil companies drill deep into the tundra ground. They hope to find oil that they can sell as fuel. When oil companies build roads and towns in the tundra, they destroy plants and disturb the animals that live there. If areas of the tundra are destroyed, plants will disappear and animals will die without food to eat.

Saving the Tundra

Each year, millions of tundra swans and arctic terns fly long distances to live on the tundra when food is plentiful. Herds of caribou raise their calves on tundra land. In the waters off the tundra, whales give birth to their young. To maintain this **diversity** of plants and animals, the tundra must be preserved.

Tundra swans raise their young on the tundra during the warm months.

Field Note

Organizations working to protect the tundra:

- Alaska Center for the Environment
- Conservation of Arctic Flora and Fauna
- World Wildlife Fund Arctic Program

Fragile Tundra Stay on Trail

Scientists and conservation workers study how development by oil companies affects the animals and plants of the tundra. They work with native people to find ways to use the land without destroying it. They try to get laws passed to limit pollution. They also teach people about the tundra biome and why it must be protected.

CHAPTER 5

Tundra Field Guide

Where to find the tundra:
northern Asia, northern Europe, northern North America

CLIMATE:

- cold and windy
- average winter temperature: minus 30 degrees Fahrenheit (minus 34 degrees Celsius)
- average summer temperature: 37 degrees to 54 degrees Fahrenheit (3 to 12 degrees Celsius)
- annual precipitation: 6 to 10 inches (15 to 25 centimeters)

INSECTS:

arctic bumblebees, black flies, crane flies, deer flies, mosquitoes, stone flies

Question:

Why might some tundra animals eat berries at certain times, when they usually eat meat?

ANIMALS:

- **Common mammals:** arctic foxes, arctic hares, arctic squirrels, caribou, ermines, lemmings, polar bears, snowshoe hares, squirrels, wolves
- **Common birds:** arctic terns, ptarmigans, snow buntings, snowy owls, tundra swans
- **Common fish:** cod, flatfish, salmon, trout

PLANTS:

arctic poppies, arctic willows, bearberries, blueberries, cloudberries, cranberries, crowberries, lichens, marsh marigolds, mosses, swamp tea

Tundra products: oil, mosses for fireworks, berries, fish

CHAPTER 6

A Scientist at Work

Ecologist Wendy Eisner lives in Ohio, but every winter she travels to Alaska to study the tundra. She drills into the frozen ground and takes out pieces of soil about the size of a broom handle. Frozen soil from deep in the ground contains **pollen** from plants that lived thousands of years ago.

In her laboratory, using a microscope, Eisner studies the pollen. She wants to identify which plants produced the pollen. Then she tries to understand how the tundra's landscape has changed over time. Her studies can help predict how the tundra will change in the future.

GLOSSARY

Arctic Circle (ARK-tik SUR-kuhl)—an imaginary line around the area of earth near the North Pole

biome (BUY-ome)—an area with a particular type of climate, and certain plants and animals that live there

climate (KLYE-mit)—the usual weather in a place

diversity (di-VUR-suh-tee)—a variety

ermine (UR-muhn)—a kind of weasel

harsh (HARSH)—unpleasant or hard

migrate (MY-grayt)—to move from one place to another and back again; birds in the Northern Hemisphere migrate by flying south in the winter, and flying back to their homes in the spring.

permafrost (PURM-uh-frawst)—ground that stays frozen year-round

pollen (POL-uhn)—tiny yellow grains that flowers produce

pollution (puh-LOO-shuhn)—harmful materials that damage the air, water, and soil

INTERNET SITES

FactHound offers a safe, fun way to find Internet sites related to this book. All of the sites on FactHound have been researched by our staff.

Here's how:

1. Visit *www.facthound.com*

2. Choose your grade level.

3. Type in this book ID **0736864083** for age-appropriate sites. You may also browse subjects by clicking on letters, or by clicking on pictures and words.

4. Click on the **Fetch It** button.

FactHound will fetch the best sites for you!

READ MORE

Baldwin, Carol. *Living in the Tundra.* Living Habitats. Chicago: Heinemann Library, 2004.

Banting, Erinn. *Tundra.* Biomes. New York: Weigl, 2006.

Butz, Christopher. *Tundra Animals.* Animals of the Biomes. Austin, Texas: Raintree Steck-Vaughn, 2002.

INDEX

ABOUT THE AUTHOR

Linda Tagliaferro

Linda Tagliaferro is an award-winning author who lives in Little Neck, New York. Linda has explored many biomes around the world. Linda has written 28 books for children, young adults, and adults. She speaks about her work at schools, libraries, and museums, such as The New York Hall of Science and New Jersey's Liberty Science Center. Her web site is www.lindatagliaferro.com.